I0012834

THE ART OF SOCIAL MEDIA CONTENT CREATION

YOUR ROAD TO SUCESS

Gospel Matthew

This book is just being made available for informational purposes. The author and publisher expressly disclaim all warranties, including without limitation warranties of fitness for a particular purpose, and make no claims or warranties about the accuracy or completeness of the contents of this book. The suggestions and tactics offered here might not be appropriate in every circumstance. Any special, incidental, consequential, or other damages of any kind resulting from or connected with the use of this book are expressly disclaimed by the author and publisher.

The accuracy of the content in this book has been carefully checked. The author and publisher, however, do not guarantee or represent at any time that the contents are correct due to the quickly changing nature of the internet and the constantly expanding nature of social media and digital marketing. This book may also contain links to websites run by third parties. These links are merely offered for convenience and in no way suggest that we approve of the goods or services that these third parties are offering. The author and publisher take no responsibility or liability for any losses or damages that may result from the use of these sites because they have no control over their content.

Cover design by Gospel Matthew

First Edition 2023

CHAPTER 1

INTRODUCTION

THE RISE OF SOCIAL MEDIA

In the not-so-distant past, the term "influencer" was virtually unheard of, and the idea of a career built on sharing your life, thoughts, and talents on the internet was but a dream. Today, the environment has undergone a significant transformation. Social media platforms have become bustling hubs of creativity, connection, and commerce, offering unprecedented opportunities for those with a passion for content creation.

Social media's meteoric rise can be attributed to a combination of factors. The widespread availability of high-speed internet, the proliferation of smartphones, and the innate human desire to connect and share have converged to create an online ecosystem that is as diverse as it is dynamic. What started as a way to reconnect with old friends or share a photo of your dinner has evolved into a multi-billion-dollar industry, with social media influencers at the forefront.

THE POWER OF CONTENT CREATION

At the heart of this digital revolution lies the concept of content creation. Content, in its myriad forms, fuels the social media engine. Whether it's a beautifully composed Instagram photo, an insightful YouTube tutorial, a clever tweet, or a heartfelt blog post, content is the currency of the internet. And those who can create compelling, engaging, and resonant content hold the keys to the kingdom.

But what exactly is content creation? It's the art of crafting and curating material for online consumption. It's about finding your unique voice, telling your story, and sharing your expertise or interests with the world. It's a journey of self-expression, creativity, and, for many, a means to build a career doing what they love.

WHAT DOES SUCCESS LOOK LIKE?

Success as a social media content creator can take many forms, and it's not always defined by the number of followers or likes you accumulate. While some creators do amass vast online audiences and significant income, others find success in different ways. It could mean connecting deeply with a niche community, creating meaningful change through advocacy, or simply finding a platform to express your thoughts and talents.

In this book, we will explore the path to becoming a successful social media content creator. Whether you're a seasoned pro looking to refine your strategies or a newcomer eager to embark on this digital adventure, this guide is designed to provide you with the knowledge, tools, and inspiration needed to thrive in the world of social media content creation.

Are you prepared to start this thrilling voyage, then? Let's dive in and discover the keys to mastering the art of social media content creation and achieving your own unique vision of success.

CHAPTER 2

FINDING YOUR NICHE

In the vast and diverse world of social media, one of the fundamental keys to success as a content creator is finding your niche. A niche is your unique corner of the digital landscape, a space where your passion, expertise, and interests intersect with an audience eager to engage with your content. In this chapter, we'll explore the process of discovering and defining your niche.

IDENTIFYING YOUR PASSIONS AND INTERESTS

Before you can carve out your niche, you must first delve into your passions and interests. Ask yourself

1. **What do I love?** Start by listing the things that genuinely excite and inspire you. Anything from cuisine and fashion to technology or travel could fall under this category.

2. **What am I knowledgeable about?** Consider your areas of expertise or subjects you've spent time learning. Your expertise can be a valuable asset in creating content that stands out.

3. **What drives my curiosity?** Sometimes, your niche might not be something you're already deeply passionate about, but rather a subject that piques your interest and motivates you to explore it further.

4. **What makes me unique?**
   Reflect on your life experiences, background, and perspective. These unique aspects of your identity can be the foundation for a niche that's distinctively yours.

Remember, finding your niche doesn't mean you're limited to a single topic forever. Many successful content creators evolve over time, expanding their niches or pivoting as their interests change or their audiences grow. The key is to start with a niche that genuinely resonates with you.

ANALYZING MARKET TRENDS

Once you've identified your passions and interests, it's essential to assess the market to determine if there's an audience for your chosen niche. Here's how

1. **Competitive Analysis** Research other content creators in your potential niche. Analyze their content, engagement rates, and audience size. Are there gaps or underserved aspects of the niche that you could fill?

2. **Keyword Research** Utilize tools like Google Keyword Planner or social media analytics platforms to identify relevant keywords and trending topics in your niche. This can help you understand what people are searching for and interested in.

3. **Audience Research** Get to know your potential audience. What are

their demographics, hobbies, and pain points? Tailoring your content to meet their needs is crucial for success.

4. **Trend Analysis** Stay updated on industry trends and emerging topics within your niche. Trends can provide valuable opportunities for timely and relevant content.

TARGET AUDIENCE RESEARCH

Understanding your target audience is paramount in niche selection. Your audience is your community, the people who will engage with, support, and grow alongside you. Consider the following

1. **Demographics** what is the age, gender, location, and socio-economic background of your ideal audience?

2. **Psychographics** Dive deeper into their interests, values, and behaviors. What motivates them? What challenges do they face?

3. **Platform Preferences** Different platforms attract different demographics. Choose the social media channels that best suit your target market.

4. **Competing Interests** Are there other niches or content creators that your target audience might also follow? Identifying these overlaps can help you tailor your content to stand out.

Finding your niche is not a one-size-fits-all process. It's a dynamic and evolving journey that requires introspection, research, and adaptability. Once you've pinpointed your niche, you're ready to embark on the next steps of your content creation journey, including building your brand and crafting your unique voice, which we'll explore in the chapters ahead.

CHAPTER 3

BUILDING YOUR BRAND

In the world of social media content creation, your brand is your identity. It's the unique essence that sets you apart from the millions of other creators vying for attention. In this chapter, we'll delve into the process of building your personal brand, a critical step on the path to becoming a successful content creator.

CREATING A UNIQUE BRAND IDENTITY

Your brand identity is the visual and emotional representation of who you are as a content creator. It encompasses several key elements

1. **Brand Name** choose a name that reflects your niche or personal identity. It should be easy to remember and available across all social media platforms.

2. **Logo and Visuals** Design a logo and establish a consistent visual theme. Your logo and color palette should resonate with your content and your audience.

3. **Voice and Tone** define your brand's voice – the style and tone of your content. Are you humorous, informative, or inspirational? Consistency in your tone helps your audience connect with you.

4. **Values and Mission** clearly articulate your values and mission. What do you stand for, and what message do you want to convey through your content?

5. **Tagline** Craft a memorable tagline or slogan that encapsulates your brand's essence.

6. **Storytelling** your personal story is a powerful tool for building your brand. Share your journey, struggles, and successes with authenticity.

CRAFTING YOUR PERSONAL STORY

Humanizing your brand through storytelling is a potent way to connect with your audience. Here's how

1. **Origin Story** Share the story of how you became interested in your niche and started creating content. Your audience will relate to your journey.

2. **Challenges and Triumphs** Be open about the challenges you've faced on your content creation journey. Highlight your successes, but also discuss how you've overcome setbacks.

3. **Vulnerability** Don't be afraid to show vulnerability. Authenticity and relatability often come from sharing your imperfections and mistakes.

4. **Passion and Purpose** Communicate why you're passionate about your niche and the purpose behind your content. Audiences are drawn to creators who genuinely care about their topics.

5. **Consistency** Maintain a consistent narrative across your content. The story you tell should align with your brand identity.

DESIGNING A MEMORABLE LOGO AND VISUALS

In order to recognize a brand, visual components are essential. Consider these tips

1. **Logo** Design a simple, memorable logo that represents your brand. It should look good in various sizes and formats.

2. **Color Palette** Choose a set of colors that resonate with your brand's personality. Consistency in color usage across your content helps with brand recognition.

3. **Typography** Select fonts that match your brand's style. Use these fonts consistently in your graphics and text overlays.

4. **Visual Style** Define a visual style for your content. This could include the types of images or graphics you use, filters, and editing techniques.

5. **Branded Templates** Create templates for your social media posts, videos, and stories. This ensures a cohesive look and feel to your content.

Building a brand is an ongoing process. As your content and audience evolve, your brand may evolve too. Regularly assess whether your brand still aligns with your goals and values, and don't be afraid to make adjustments as needed.

Your brand is what makes you recognizable and memorable in the crowded social media landscape. In the chapters ahead, we'll explore how to use this brand to create a cohesive content strategy and engage with your audience effectively.

CHAPTER 4

CONTENT PLANNING AND STRATEGY

Creating captivating and purposeful content is at the core of being a successful social media content creator. In this chapter, we'll dive into the importance of content planning and strategy, helping you develop a systematic approach to producing content that resonates with your audience.

SETTING GOALS AND OBJECTIVES

Setting up clear goals and objectives is essential before starting to create content.

Your objectives will direct your content strategy and assist you in determining success. Consider the following

1. **Audience Growth** Are you looking to increase your follower count, subscribers, or overall reach?

2. **Engagement** Do you want to foster more interactions, such as likes, comments, and shares, with your audience?

3. **Brand Partnerships** Are you seeking to collaborate with brands or secure sponsorships?

4. **Monetization** Is your primary goal to generate income from your content through methods like affiliate

marketing, product sales, or ad revenue?

5. **Educational or Inspirational** Do you aim to educate, inspire, or entertain your audience on specific topics?

6. **Advocacy** Are you passionate about a particular cause or issue, and do you want to use your platform for advocacy?

By defining your objectives, you'll have a clear direction for your content strategy.

CONTENT CALENDAR AND SCHEDULING

In the realm of social media, consistency is crucial. Creating a content calendar and scheduling your posts in advance can help you maintain a regular posting schedule. Here's how to get started

1. **Content Categories** Categorize your content into themes or topics that align with your niche and goals. This can help you diversify your content while staying focused.

2. **Posting Frequency** Determine how often you'll post on each platform. It's essential to find a balance that suits your audience and aligns with your capacity.

3. **Timing** Research when your target audience is most active on social media, and schedule your posts during those peak times.

4. **Content Types** Plan a mix of content types, such as photos, videos, stories, and written posts, to keep your feed engaging and varied.

5. **Holidays and Trends** Incorporate relevant holidays and trending topics into your content calendar when appropriate.

6. **Evergreen vs. Timely Content** Strike a balance between evergreen content (content that remains relevant over time) and timely content (related to current events or trends).

BALANCING DIFFERENT CONTENT TYPES

Diversifying your content can keep your audience engaged and attract a broader range of followers. Consider incorporating the following content types into your strategy

1. **Educational Content** Share your expertise and knowledge on topics related to your niche.

2. **Behind-the-Scenes** Give your audience a glimpse of your daily life, creative process, or workspace.

3. **Interactive Content** Run polls, quizzes, or Q&A sessions to engage with your audience directly.

4. **User-Generated Content** Encourage your followers to create content related to your niche and share it on your platform.

5. **Storytelling** Share personal anecdotes, success stories, or narratives that resonate with your audience.

6. **Collaborations** Partner with other creators, brands, or influencers for co-created content.

7. **Product Reviews** If relevant, provide honest reviews of products or services related to your niche.

8. **Inspirational or Motivational Content** Share messages of encouragement and positivity.

Remember that the key to a successful content strategy is authenticity. Your content should align with your brand and values while catering to your audience's interests and needs.

As you plan and strategize your content, always stay open to feedback and adapt your approach based on what resonates most with your audience. In the chapters ahead, we'll explore techniques for creating compelling content and optimizing it for different social media platforms.

CHAPTER 5

CONTENT CREATION TECHNIQUES

Creating high-quality content is the lifeblood of your social media presence. In this chapter, we'll explore various content creation techniques to help you craft engaging and visually appealing posts that resonate with your audience.

PHOTOGRAPHY AND VIDEOGRAPHY TIPS

PHOTOGRAPHY

1. **Lighting** Good lighting is essential for great photos. Natural light often

works best, so consider shooting near windows during the day. Avoid harsh shadows.

2. **Composition** Use the rule of thirds to frame your subject, and experiment with angles and perspectives for unique shots.

3. **Background** Choose backgrounds that complement your subject and don't distract from it. A clean, uncluttered background can make your subject pop.

4. **Editing** Edit your photos to enhance colors, contrast, and sharpness. There are numerous photo editing apps available to help with this.

5. **Props and Styling** Props can add depth and interest to your photos. Experiment with different props that align with your niche.

VIDEOGRAPHY

1. **Steady Shots** Invest in a tripod or stabilizer to keep your videos steady. Shaky footage can be distracting.

2. **Audio Quality** Good audio is as important as video quality. Use an external microphone when possible to capture clear sound.

3. **Storytelling** Plan your video content with a clear beginning, middle, and end. Storytelling keeps your audience engaged.

4. **B-Roll Footage** Incorporate supplementary shots (B-roll) to add visual interest and context to your videos.

5. **Editing** Edit your videos to remove unnecessary parts, add transitions, and enhance audio. Video editing software can be powerful tools.

GRAPHIC DESIGN BASICS

Creating eye-catching graphics is vital for many social media platforms. Here are some graphic design principles to consider

1. **Color Theory** Understand the psychology of colors and use them to evoke specific emotions or associations in your audience.

2. **Typography** Choose fonts that are easy to read and match your brand's style. Experiment with font pairings for visual contrast.

3. **Whitespace** Don't overcrowd your designs. Leave enough whitespace to make your content visually appealing and legible.

4. **Consistency** Use consistent design elements, such as colors and fonts, across your graphics to reinforce your brand identity.

5. **Visual Hierarchy** Highlight the most important information or elements in your design. Use size, color, or placement to create hierarchy.

6. **Balance** Achieve visual balance by distributing elements evenly throughout your design.

7. **Simplicity** Keep your designs simple and focused to convey your message clearly.

WRITING ENGAGING

CAPTIONS

Your captions can enhance the impact of your content. Here's how to write engaging captions

1. **Hook** Start with an attention-grabbing opening line to draw readers in.

2. **Storytelling** Share anecdotes, personal experiences, or narratives that relate to your content.

3. **Ask Questions** Encourage interaction by asking open-ended questions that invite comments.

4. **Use Emoji's** Emoji's can add personality and emotion to your captions.

5. **Call to Action (CTA)** encourage your audience to take specific actions, such as liking, sharing, or visiting your website.

6. **Hashtags** Use relevant hashtags to increase the discoverability of your posts. Research popular hashtags in your niche.

7. **Length** Find the right balance between short and long captions. Some posts may benefit from brevity, while others require more context.

8. **Editing** proofread your captions for spelling and grammatical errors. Clear and error-free text adds professionalism to your content.

Remember, the key to effective content creation is practice and continuous improvement. Experiment with different techniques, gather feedback from your audience, and refine your approach over time. In the following chapters, we'll explore strategies for navigating social media platforms and engaging with your audience effectively.

CHAPTER 6

PLATFORMS AND ALGORITHMS

In the ever-evolving landscape of social media, understanding the various platforms and the algorithms that govern them is crucial for a content creator's success. In this chapter, we'll explore different social media platforms and provide insights into how their algorithms work.

UNDERSTANDING DIFFERENT SOCIAL MEDIA PLATFORMS

1. Instagram Visual Storytelling

Strengths Ideal for visual content, photography, and lifestyle niches.

Features Instagram Stories, IGTV, Reels, and a grid-style feed.

Audience Predominantly younger, with a strong focus on visuals and aesthetics.

2. YouTube Video Dominance

Strengths The go-to platform for video content and tutorials.

Features Longer video format, live streaming, and monetization options.

Audience Diverse, ranging from educational content seekers to entertainment enthusiasts.

Twitter Real-Time Updates

Strengths Quick updates, news sharing, and trending topics.

Features 280-character limit, hashtags, and retweets.

Audience Varied, including journalists, influencers, and everyday users seeking real-time information.

1. Facebook Broad Reach

- **Strengths** Wide audience reach, groups, and pages for specific interests.

- **Features** Text, images, videos, and live streaming.

- **Audience** Diverse age groups and

CHAPTER 7

AUDIENCE ENGAGEMENT

Building and sustaining a loyal and engaged audience is at the heart of success as a social media content creator. In this chapter, we'll delve into strategies for fostering meaningful connections with your audience, driving interaction, and cultivating a vibrant online community.

RESPONDING TO COMMENTS AND MESSAGES

Engagement often begins with a simple act responding to comments and messages. Here's how to do it effectively

1. **Timeliness** Aim to respond promptly. Quick responses demonstrate how much you appreciate the opinions of your audience.
2. **Personalization** Address people by their names whenever possible. Personalized responses make your audience feel heard and appreciated.

3. **Authenticity** Be genuine in your responses. Authenticity fosters trust and deeper connections.

4. **Encourage Conversation** Pose questions or ask for opinions in your replies to encourage further discussion.

5. **Handle Criticism Gracefully** Not all comments will be positive. Handle criticism with professionalism and empathy.

6. **Set Boundaries** While engagement is essential, it's okay to set boundaries and manage your time effectively.

HOSTING Q&A SESSIONS AND LIVE STREAMS

Live interactions can be powerful tools for engagement. Consider these approaches

1. **Q&A Sessions** Host live question-and-answer sessions to directly interact with your audience. It's an

opportunity to provide insights and share your expertise.

2. **Live Streams** Go live to share real-time moments, behind-the-scenes glimpses, or to discuss trending topics. Live streams encourage immediate engagement through comments and reactions.

3. **Announcements and Updates** Use live sessions to make important announcements or updates, fostering a sense of community involvement.

4. **Collaborations** Collaborate with other creators for joint live streams, broadening your reach and introducing your audience to new voices.

RUNNING CONTESTS AND GIVEAWAYS

Contests and giveaways can inject excitement into your content and boost engagement

1. **Clear Rules** Set clear rules and guidelines for participation. Transparency is crucial to build trust.

2. **Prizes** Offer enticing prizes that resonate with your audience's interests or needs.

3. **Engagement Requirements** Encourage likes, shares, comments, or user-generated content as entry requirements.

4. **Promotion** Promote your contest or giveaway across your social media channels and leverage relevant hashtags.

5. **Winner Selection** Select winners fairly and publicly announce them. Consider using tools for randomized selection.

HOSTING AMAS (ASK ME ANYTHING)

AMAs are interactive sessions where your audience can ask you anything. They create a sense of intimacy and transparency. Here's how to conduct a successful AMA

1. **Announcement** Promote your AMA session in advance to build anticipation.

2. **Diverse Topics** Be open to a wide range of questions. This encourages active participation.

3. **Preparation** Have key points or topics ready, but also be spontaneous and open to unexpected questions.

4. **Moderation** Consider using moderators to filter and organize questions, especially if you anticipate a large audience.

GAMIFY ENGAGEMENT

Gamification techniques, such as challenges or quizzes, can ignite engagement

1. **Challenges** Create challenges related to your niche or interests. Encourage your audience to participate and share their results.

2. **Quizzes and Polls** Use polls and quizzes to spark interaction. People love expressing their opinions and testing their knowledge.

3. **Leaderboards** Consider recognizing top commenters or most engaged followers to incentivize participation.

Remember, the goal of audience engagement is not only to boost metrics like likes and comments but also to create meaningful connections and a sense of community around your content. Consistency, authenticity, and a genuine interest in your audience's needs and opinions are the keys to fostering lasting engagement. In the following chapters, we'll explore analytics and data-driven strategies to further refine your content and engagement efforts.

CHAPTER 8

COLLABORATIONS AND NETWORKING

Collaborations and networking are essential strategies for expanding your reach, gaining new perspectives, and strengthening your position as a social media content creator. In this chapter, we'll explore the power of collaborating with others in your field and building a network that can help you thrive.

BUILDING RELATIONSHIPS WITH OTHER CREATORS

It can be advantageous for both parties to collaborate with other content developers. Here's how to build those essential relationships

1. **Identify Potential Collaborators** Seek out creators whose content aligns with your niche or complements your own. Look for shared values and interests.

2. **Reach Out Professionally** Initiate contact with a friendly, professional approach. Explain your ideas for collaboration and the potential benefits for both parties.

3. **Collaboration Ideas** Brainstorm creative collaboration ideas, such as joint videos, guest appearances, or co-created content.

4. **Clear Communication** Maintain clear communication throughout the collaboration process, including expectations, timelines, and division of tasks.

5. **Mutual Promotion** Promote each other's content on your respective platforms, broadening your reach to each other's audiences.

6. **Long-Term Relationships** Building lasting collaborations can lead to enduring partnerships and friendships within the content creator community.

PARTNERING WITH BRANDS AND INFLUENCERS

Collaborating with brands and influencers can open new opportunities for monetization and audience growth

1. **Brand Alignment** Partner with brands whose values align with your own and resonate with your audience.

2. **Authenticity** Maintain authenticity when promoting products or services. Your audience trusts your recommendations.

3. **Contracts and Agreements** Clearly define the terms of your partnership in contracts or agreements, including

compensation, deliverables, and timelines.

4. **Disclosure** Always disclose partnerships and sponsorships to maintain transparency with your audience.

5. **Creative Control** Negotiate creative control to ensure the content aligns with your brand and style.

6. **Long-Term Partnerships** Seek long-term partnerships with brands to build trust and consistency.

NETWORKING EVENTS AND CONFERENCES

Networking events and conferences offer valuable opportunities to connect with others in your industry

1. **Research Events** Identify industry-specific events, conferences, and meetups relevant to your niche.

2. **Prepare Elevator Pitch** Craft a concise elevator pitch that introduces you and your content to potential connections.

3. **Engage Actively** Attend sessions, engage in discussions, and participate in networking activities to make meaningful connections.

4. **Exchange Contact Information** Collect business cards or exchange

social media profiles to stay in touch with new contacts.

5. **Follow up after** the event, follow up with your new connections through emails or social media messages.

6. **Leverage Online Communities** Join online forums or groups related to your niche to extend your networking efforts.

7. **Stay Updated** Continuously update your knowledge by attending industry events regularly.

Remember, networking is not just about what you can gain; it's also about what you can offer to others. Building genuine relationships within your industry can lead to opportunities, collaborations, and valuable insights that benefit both you and your network.

In the chapters ahead, we'll delve into data-driven strategies and monetization techniques, empowering you to refine your content creation skills and maximize your success as a social media content creator.

CHAPTER 9

ANALYTICS AND DATA

In the world of social media content creation, data is your compass. Understanding your audience's preferences, tracking your progress, and making data-driven decisions are vital for long-term success. In this chapter, we'll explore the importance of analytics and data in your content creation journey.

TRACKING KEY METRICS

Before diving into the intricacies of analytics, it's crucial to identify and understand the key metrics that matter most to your goals. Some common metrics include

1. **Follower Growth** Monitoring the growth of your audience over time is a fundamental metric. It indicates the health of your content strategy and marketing efforts.

2. **Engagement Rate** Measuring likes, comments, shares, and saves can help you gauge the level of interaction your content generates.

3. **Reach and Impressions** These metrics tell you how many people have seen your content and how often. Reach is the total number of unique viewers, while impressions count all views, including multiple views by the same user.

4. **Click-Through Rate (CTR)** In the context of links or call-to-action buttons, CTR measures the percentage of users who clicked compared to those who saw the link.

5. **Conversion Rate** If your goal is to drive actions like signing up for a newsletter or making a purchase, this rate tells you how many users completed the desired action.

6. **Audience Demographics** Understanding your audience's age, gender, location, and interests can help tailor your content.

7. **Content Performance** Analyze which types of content (e.g., photos,

videos, blog posts) perform best and adapt your strategy accordingly.

8. **Time Metrics** Know when your audience is most active to optimize your posting schedule.

USING ANALYTICS TOOLS

A plethora of analytics tools are available for content creators to gather and analyze data. Here are a few popular options

1. **Platform Analytics** Most social media platforms offer built-in analytics tools that provide insights into your account's performance. For example, Instagram Insights and YouTube Analytics.

2. **Google Analytics** if you have a website or blog, Google Analytics can track website traffic, user behavior, and conversion rates.

3. **Third-Party Tools** Tools like Hoot suite, Buffer, and Sprout Social offer advanced analytics, scheduling, and content planning features.

4. **Custom Tracking** You can set up custom tracking using UTM parameters to monitor specific marketing campaigns or links.

ADJUSTING YOUR STRATEGY BASED ON DATA

The real value of data lies in your ability to adapt and improve your content strategy based on what you learn. Here's how

1. **Identify Trends** Regularly review your analytics to identify trends and patterns. What type of content gets the most engagement? When is your audience most active?

2. **A/B Testing** Experiment with different content styles, posting times, and messaging to see what resonates best with your audience.

3. **Content Calendar Adjustments** Use data to refine your content calendar. When you think your audience will be online, schedule content for certain times.

4. **Audience Targeting** Tailor your content to specific audience segments based on their demographics and interests.

5. **Goal Setting** Set specific, measurable, and achievable goals based on your analytics data. Keep track of your development toward achieving these objectives.

6. **Stay Updated** Social media platforms and algorithms change frequently. Stay informed about updates and adapt your strategy accordingly.

7. **Competitive Analysis** Analyze your competitors' content and strategies to identify opportunities for improvement.

Remember that data is a tool to guide your decisions, but it should be used in conjunction with your creativity and intuition. Striking a balance between data-driven strategies and authentic content creation is key to your long-term success as a social media content creator.

In the following chapters, we'll explore monetization strategies, legal and ethical considerations, and provide practical tips for maintaining authenticity and avoiding burnout.

CHAPTER 10

MONETIZATION STRATEGIES

Monetization is the process of turning your passion for content creation into a sustainable income. In this chapter, we'll explore various monetization strategies that can help you generate revenue from your social media efforts.

AFFILIATE MARKETING

Affiliate marketing is a popular monetization method where you promote products or services and earn a commission for every sale generated through your unique affiliate link. Here's how to get started

1. **Choose Relevant Products** Select products or services that align with your niche and resonate with your audience.

2. **Join Affiliate Programs** Sign up for affiliate programs offered by companies and brands. Many businesses have dedicated affiliate programs you can join.

3. **Create Honest Reviews** Craft in-depth, honest reviews or recommendations of the products or services you're promoting.

4. **Transparent Disclosure** Always disclose your affiliate relationships to maintain transparency with your audience.

5. **Track Your Performance** Use affiliate tracking tools to monitor your conversions and earnings. This data can help you refine your strategies.

6. **Quality over Quantity** Focus on promoting products that genuinely provide value to your audience. Quality recommendations build trust.

SPONSORED POSTS AND BRAND DEALS

In sponsored posts, brands are partnered with to provide content that promotes their goods or services. Here's how to secure sponsored opportunities

1. **Build a Strong Online Presence** Brands are more likely to collaborate with content creators who have a significant and engaged following.

2. **Identify Brand Fit** Partner with brands that align with your niche and resonate with your audience.

3. **Pitch Your Ideas** Reach out to brands with well-thought-out proposals for collaboration. Highlight the value you can offer.

4. **Negotiate Terms** Negotiate terms and compensation that reflect your audience's size and engagement.

5. **Deliver High-Quality Content** Create sponsored content that

seamlessly integrates the brand's message with your own unique style.

6. **Disclosure and Transparency** Always disclose sponsored content to maintain trust with your audience.

SELLING MERCHANDISE AND DIGITAL PRODUCTS

Creating and selling your merchandise or digital products can be a lucrative way to monetize your brand. Here's how to get started

1. **Design Unique Merchandise** Create branded merchandise that resonates with your audience. This could include clothing, accessories, or other physical items.

2. **Leverage Print-on-Demand Services** Use print-on-demand services to avoid upfront production costs. These services print and ship products as orders come in.

3. **Digital Products** Offer digital products like e-books, online courses, presets, or templates related to your niche.

4. **Set up an Online Store create** an online store on your website or use e-commerce platforms like Shopify or Etsy.

5. **Promote Your Products** Promote your merchandise and digital products through your social media channels and email marketing.

6. **Engage Your Audience** Highlight the benefits of your products and engage with your audience to answer questions and build excitement.

DONATIONS AND CROWDFUNDING

Some content creators rely on donations and crowdfunding from their audience to support their work. This can include platforms like Patreon, Ko-fi, or even direct donations through platforms like PayPal.

1. **Offer Value** Provide exclusive content or perks to your supporters, such as early access, behind-the-scenes content, or personalized shutouts.

2. **Communicate Goals** Clearly communicate how donations will support your content creation and what your supporters can expect in return.

3. **Show Appreciation** Regularly express your gratitude to your supporters and involve them in your content creation process.

DIVERSIFY YOUR INCOME STREAMS

To ensure long-term financial stability, consider diversifying your income streams. Relying on a single method may leave you vulnerable to changes in the market or platform policies. Experiment with various monetization strategies to find what works best for you and your audience.

Remember, successful monetization often comes with time and persistence. Building trust with your audience and consistently delivering value should remain at the core of your content creation efforts. In the following chapters, we'll explore legal and ethical considerations, maintaining authenticity, and strategies for overcoming challenges such as burnout.

CHAPTER 11

LEGAL AND ETHICAL CONSIDERATIONS

As a social media content creator, it's crucial to navigate the legal and ethical aspects of the digital landscape. This chapter will guide you through some of the key considerations to ensure you operate within the bounds of the law and maintain ethical standards in your content creation journey.

COPYRIGHT AND INTELLECTUAL PROPERTY

Respect for intellectual property rights is fundamental in content creation

1. **Understand Copyright** Familiarize yourself with copyright laws in your country. Copyright protects original creative works like text, images, music, and videos.

2. **Use Licensed Content** Obtain proper licenses or permissions when using copyrighted material in your content. Creative Commons licenses and stock photo sites can be valuable resources.

3. **Fair Use** Familiarize yourself with fair use guidelines, which may allow limited use of copyrighted material for purposes like criticism, commentary, news reporting, or education. Always attribute the source when applicable.

4. **Protect Your Work** Take steps to protect your own content from unauthorized use. Watermarking images or using digital rights management (DRM) for digital products can help.

PRIVACY AND DATA PROTECTION

Observe people's rights to privacy and data protection

1. **Obtain Consent** Always obtain proper consent before using someone's likeness, name, or personal information in your content. This includes individuals in photos or videos and anyone you interview.

2. **Data Collection** Clearly disclose your data collection practices,

including the use of cookies and the handling of personal information on your website or platform.

3. **Comply with GDPR** If you have a global audience, be aware of and comply with regulations like the General Data Protection Regulation (GDPR) if applicable.

4. **Children's Privacy** familiarize yourself with regulations like COPPA (Children's Online Privacy Protection Act) and ensure compliance when your content is targeted at children.

SPONSORED CONTENT AND DISCLOSURES

Maintain transparency in your content, especially when it involves sponsorship or partnerships

1. **Disclosures** Clearly disclose any sponsored content or affiliate relationships to your audience. Use labels like ad, sponsored, or affiliate.

2. **Honest Reviews** Ensure that your reviews and recommendations, even in sponsored content, remain honest and unbiased. Your audience trusts your authenticity.

3. **FTC Guidelines** Familiarize yourself with the Federal Trade Commission (FTC) guidelines for endorsements and testimonials.

Content Moderation and Community Guidelines

Most social media platforms have community guidelines that you must adhere to

1. **Read and Follow Guidelines** Review and follow the guidelines of the platforms you use. These rules can be broken, and the content may be removed or the account suspended.
2. **Moderate Comments** Actively moderate comments on your content to remove offensive or harmful content. For your audience, provide a welcoming and secure environment.
3. **Report Abuse** Report abusive or harmful behavior to the platform authorities. Your vigilance can help protect your audience.

ETHICAL CONTENT CREATION

Maintaining ethical standards in your content creation is essential for long-term credibility and trust

1. **Fact-Check** Ensure the accuracy of any information you present. Misinformation can damage your reputation.

2. **Avoid Hate Speech and Discrimination** Steer clear of hate speech, discrimination, or any content that promotes harm or prejudice against individuals or groups.

3. **Respect Cultural Sensitivities** Be aware of and respectful towards

cultural sensitivities and differences. In certain cultures, what is acceptable could not be in others.

4. **Use Your Influence Responsibly** Understand the impact you have on your audience. Use your platform to promote positive messages and causes.

5. **Be Mindful of Trends** Be cautious when jumping on trends or challenges. Ensure they align with your values and are not harmful or offensive.

Navigating the legal and ethical aspects of content creation requires ongoing diligence and a commitment to upholding high standards. Always prioritize honesty, transparency, and the well-being of your audience. In the following chapters, we'll explore strategies for maintaining authenticity and overcoming challenges such as burnout.

CHAPTER 12

AUTHENTICITY AND BUILDING TRUST

Authenticity is the cornerstone of a successful social media content creator's journey. For long-term success, developing trust with your audience is essential. In this chapter, we'll delve into the significance of authenticity and provide strategies for cultivating genuine connections with your followers.

THE POWER OF AUTHENTICITY

Authenticity means being true to yourself, transparent, and honest in your content. Here's why it matters

1. **Building Trust** Authenticity builds trust with your audience. When your audience believes in your sincerity, they're more likely to engage and stay loyal.

2. **Differentiation** In a crowded online space, authenticity sets you apart. Your unique voice and perspective become your signature.

3. **Connection** Authenticity fosters deeper connections. Your audience can relate to your struggles, journey, and values.

4. **Resilience** Authentic creators are more resilient to criticism and negative feedback. Trust helps you weather challenges.

STRATEGIES FOR AUTHENTIC CONTENT CREATION

1. **Know Your Values** Understand your core values and let them guide your content. Your beliefs should shine through in your posts.

2. **Share Your Journey** Be open about your journey, including both successes and failures. This humanizes you and makes your story relatable.

3. **3. Accept Vulnerability** Don't be ashamed to display vulnerability. Sharing your imperfections can help your audience connect with you on a deeper level.

4. **Engage Authentically** Interact with your audience genuinely. Authenticity and thankfulness should be used while answering comments and messages.

5. **Be Consistent** Consistency in your messaging and tone helps reinforce your authenticity. Avoid making abrupt adjustments that could mislead your readers.

6. **Share Real-Life Moments** Document real-life moments, challenges, and experiences. Authenticity often comes from the everyday.

OVERCOMING THE FEAR OF VULNERABILITY

Sharing your authentic self can be intimidating, but it's essential for building trust

1. **Start Small** If you're uncomfortable with vulnerability, start with small, personal stories or insights.

2. **Remind Yourself of the Why** Remember why you started creating content. Your message and mission should drive you to be authentic.

3. **Audience Connection** Understand that vulnerability often deepens the

connection between you and your audience.

4. **Accept Imperfection** You don't need to have all the answers or be perfect. Your audience appreciates your authenticity and growth.

Handling Criticism and Negativity

Authenticity can sometimes attract criticism. Here's how to navigate it

1. **Constructive Feedback** Distinguish between constructive criticism and baseless negativity. Use feedback for growth when it's valuable.

2. **Maintain Grace** Respond to criticism with grace and professionalism. Avoid engaging in online conflicts.

3. **Lean on Your Community** Your loyal audience can be a source of support when you face negativity. They often rally behind authentic creators.

4. **Boundaries** Set boundaries for yourself. You don't have to share everything. Your well-being matters.

CONSISTENCY IS KEY

Consistency is vital in maintaining authenticity. How to be true to yourself over time is as follows

1. **Regular Self-Reflection** Periodically reflect on your values and goals. This helps you stay aligned with your authentic self.

2. **Audience Feedback** Pay attention to your audience's feedback. They can help keep you accountable to your authenticity.

3. **Evolution is Natural** Understand that you'll evolve over time. Your authenticity should evolve with you.

4. **Trust the Process** Building authenticity takes time. Trust that staying true to yourself will yield positive results in the long run.

Authenticity is a journey, not a destination. It's a continuous commitment to being genuine, transparent, and true to your values. Accept your individuality and let it come over in your content. In the following chapters, we'll explore strategies for overcoming challenges like burnout and maintaining your passion for content creation.

CHAPTER 13

OVERCOMING CHALLENGES AND SUSTAINING PASSION

As a social media content creator, you'll encounter various challenges along your journey. It's essential to address these challenges and maintain your passion for content creation. In this chapter, we'll explore common obstacles and strategies for overcoming them.

RECOGNIZING COMMON CHALLENGES

1. **Content Burnout** The pressure to consistently create content can lead to burnout, resulting in decreased creativity and motivation.

2. **Audience Engagement Fluctuations** Audience engagement may vary, causing frustration during low-engagement periods.

3. **Comparison and Imposter Syndrome** Comparing yourself to others can lead to self-doubt and imposter syndrome.

4. **Monetization Pressures** The pressure to monetize your content may affect your authenticity and creativity.

5. **Algorithm Changes** Social media algorithms are dynamic, impacting your content's reach and visibility.

6. **Negativity and Trolls** Dealing with negativity and trolls can be emotionally draining.

STRATEGIES FOR OVERCOMING CHALLENGES

1. **Set Realistic Goals** Establish achievable content creation goals and timelines to avoid burnout. Quality content matters more than quantity.

2. **Diversify Your Content** Experiment with new content

formats, topics, or platforms to rekindle your creativity and engage your audience.

3. **Engage with Your Audience** Actively engage with your audience and seek their input. Feedback can provide valuable insights and motivation.

4. **Practice Self-Compassion** Be kind to yourself. Understand that everyone faces challenges, and it's okay to take breaks when needed.

5. **Limit Comparison** Focus on your journey rather than comparing yourself to others. Recognize that everyone's path is unique.

6. **Monetize Mindfully** Prioritize authenticity and ethics in your monetization strategies. Don't compromise your values for financial gain.

7. **Stay Informed** Keep up with industry trends and algorithm changes. Adapt your strategy accordingly.

8. **Develop a Support System** Connect with fellow content creators or seek support from friends and family during challenging times.

CULTIVATING AND SUSTAINING PASSION

Maintaining your passion is essential for long-term success

1. **Rediscover Your Why** Reflect on why you started creating content in the first place. Reconnect with your initial passion.

2. **Explore New Interests** Allow your interests to evolve and incorporate them into your content. This keeps your creative spark alive.

3. **Take Breaks** Regularly schedule breaks to recharge and prevent burnout. Vacations and digital detoxes can be rejuvenating.

4. **Continuous Learning** Stay curious and open to learning. Exploring new skills or knowledge can reignite your passion.

5. **Collaborate and Network** Collaborating with others can bring fresh perspectives and excitement to your content.

6. **Celebrate Milestones** Celebrate your achievements and milestones, no matter how small. Recognize your progress.

Seek Professional Help if Needed

If you're struggling with mental health issues related to content creation, consider seeking professional help. Mental health is paramount, and there's no shame in seeking support from therapists or counselors.

Remember that challenges are a natural part of the content creation journey. By acknowledging them and implementing strategies to overcome them, you can sustain your passion, creativity, and authenticity in the world of social media content creation.

In the final chapters, we'll explore the future of content creation, the evolving landscape of social media, and ways to adapt and thrive in this dynamic field.

CHAPTER 14

THE FUTURE OF CONTENT CREATION

The landscape of content creation is ever-evolving, shaped by emerging technologies, changing audience behaviors, and platform developments. In this chapter, we'll explore the future trends and potential shifts that content creators should be aware of to stay relevant and successful in the years to come.

1. VIDEO DOMINANCE

Video content is poised to continue its dominance in the content creation landscape.

Live streaming, short-form videos, and interactive content are all growing in popularity. To thrive

- **Master Video Creation** Hone your video creation skills, including editing, storytelling, and live streaming techniques.

- **Adapt to Short-Form Content** Platforms like TikTok and Instagram Reels reward concise, engaging content.

- **Explore Live Streaming** Live streams foster real-time engagement and can help you connect with your audience on a deeper level.

2. AUGMENTED REALITY (AR) AND VIRTUAL REALITY (VR)

Immersive and interactive experiences are being offered through AR and VR technologies, which are increasing popularity. Content creators can leverage these technologies in various ways

- **AR Filters and Lenses** Create custom AR filters or lenses for platforms like Instagram and Snapchat to engage your audience in novel ways.

- **360-Degree Videos** Experiment with 360-degree videos to offer immersive storytelling experiences.

- **VR Content** As VR becomes more accessible, explore creating content designed for VR headsets.

3. ARTIFICIAL INTELLIGENCE (AI)

AI-driven content creation tools are becoming more sophisticated. AI can assist content creators in

- **Content Generation** AI can generate text, images, and even videos, potentially streamlining content creation.

- **Data Analysis** Use AI-powered analytics tools to gain deeper insights into your audience and content performance.

4. NICHE AND MICRO-INFLUENCERS

The era of mega-influencers may give way to niche and micro-influencers who have smaller but highly engaged and loyal followings. Focus on

- **Niche Expertise** Become an authority in your niche to attract a dedicated audience.

- **Authenticity** Maintain authenticity in your content to build trust with your followers.

5. EPHEMERAL CONTENT

Ephemeral content, which disappears after a short period, continues to rise in popularity. Platforms like Snapchat and Instagram Stories rely heavily on this format. To excel

- **Master Storytelling** Craft engaging narratives within the limited timeframe.

- **Promote Urgency** Leverage the temporary nature of ephemeral content to drive immediate actions like limited-time offers.

6. PRIVACY AND DATA PROTECTION

As concerns about data privacy grow, content creators must prioritize ethical data practices

- **Transparency** Clearly communicate your data collection and usage policies to your audience.

- **Compliance** Stay informed about and comply with evolving data protection regulations like GDPR and CCPA.

7. MULTICHANNEL PRESENCE

Diversifying your presence across multiple platforms can enhance your resilience to algorithm changes or platform instability

- Cross-Promotion Promote your content on various platforms to reach different audiences.

- **Platform Expertise** Understand the nuances of each platform to tailor your content effectively.

8. SUSTAINABLE AND RESPONSIBLE CONTENT

Audiences increasingly value sustainability and social responsibility. Consider

1. **Sustainable Practices** Highlight eco-friendly and sustainable practices in your content if relevant to your niche.

2. **Social Causes** Use your platform to raise awareness and support social causes that align with your values.

The future of content creation promises exciting opportunities and challenges. By staying informed, embracing new technologies, and remaining true to your authentic voice, you can navigate the evolving landscape and continue to create meaningful and impactful content for your audience.

In the final chapter, we'll recap the key takeaways and offer some parting thoughts for your content creation journey.

CHAPTER 15

CONCLUSION

PARTING THOUGHTS AND KEY TAKEAWAYS

Congratulations on embarking on your journey as a social media content creator! As you've explored the various aspects of this dynamic field, we've covered a wide range of topics to help you succeed and thrive. In this final chapter, let's recap some key takeaways and offer parting thoughts to guide you on your ongoing adventure.

KEY TAKEAWAYS

1. **Authenticity is King** Authenticity builds trust and connection with your audience. Stay true to your values and be genuine in your content.

2. **Know Your Audience** Understand your audience's interests, preferences, and pain points. Make sure your material is relevant to their needs.

3. **Content Quality Matters** Prioritize quality over quantity. Engaging, informative, or entertaining content will always attract and retain an audience.

4. **Consistency is Key** Maintain a consistent posting schedule to keep your audience engaged and coming back for more.

5. **Diversify Your Skills** Develop a range of skills, from content creation to analytics, to adapt to the ever-changing landscape.

6. **Monetize Mindfully** While monetization is essential, prioritize ethical and authentic monetization strategies that align with your brand.

7. **Stay Informed** Keep up with industry trends, platform changes, and evolving technologies to remain competitive.

8. **Engage Actively** Foster a sense of community by actively engaging with your audience, responding to comments, and seeking their input.

9. **Overcome Challenges** Challenges are part of the journey. Gain adaptability and resilience to overcome challenges.

10. **Passion Fuels Creativity** Your passion for your niche is your greatest asset. Nurture it, stay curious, and keep learning.

PARTING THOUGHTS

Your journey as a content creator is a unique adventure filled with opportunities for growth, creativity, and impact. It's a journey that evolves as you do, and it can be incredibly rewarding.

Remember that success in content creation is not just about metrics and numbers; it's about the meaningful connections you make with your audience and the positive impact you have on their lives.

Stay true to your vision, embrace change, and keep pushing the boundaries of your creativity. Surround yourself with a supportive community of fellow creators and mentors who can inspire and guide you along the way.

Your voice, your perspective, and your authenticity are what make your content unique. Keep creating, keep learning, and enjoy the incredible journey of being a social media content creator. The digital world is your canvas, and the possibilities are endless.

Best of luck, and may your content continue to inspire, educate, and entertain!

APPENDIX

ADDITIONAL RESOURCES

In your journey as a social media content creator, you'll find valuable resources that can further enhance your skills and knowledge. Here's a curated list of resources to help you navigate the world of content creation effectively

1. ONLINE COURSES AND PLATFORMS

- **Coursera** Offers a wide range of courses on digital marketing, content creation, and social media management.

- **Udemy** Provides numerous courses on video production, social media marketing, and content strategy.

- **edX** Features courses from top universities and institutions, including digital marketing and social media-related topics.

2. BOOKS

- **"Contagious** How to Build Word of Mouth in the Digital Age" by Jonah Berger explores the psychology behind viral content and how to create it?

- **"Jab, Jab, Jab, Right Hook** How to Tell Your Story in a Noisy Social World" by Gary Vaynerchuk Offers insights into effective social media content strategies.

- **"Building a StoryBrand** Clarify Your Message So Customers Will Listen" by Donald Miller Focuses on crafting compelling narratives for your brand.

3. ONLINE COMMUNITIES AND FORUMS

- **Reedit** Explore subedits like r/social media and r/content creators for discussions, tips, and networking.

- **Quota** Join relevant topics and engage with industry experts and fellow creators.

- **Digital Marketing and Content Creation Facebook Groups** Many groups cater to content creators and digital marketers, offering support and advice.

4. TOOLS AND SOFTWARE

- **Canva** A user-friendly graphic design tool for creating visually appealing content.

- **Buffer** A social media management platform that allows you to schedule and analyze your content.

- **Hoot suite** another popular social media management tool with scheduling and analytics features.

5. YOUTUBE CHANNELS AND PODCASTS

- **Neil Patel** Offers insightful digital marketing and content creation tips.

- **The Content Creator Podcast** Explores various aspects of content creation and storytelling.

- **GaryVee Audio Experience** Gary Vaynerchuk shares his expertise in marketing, entrepreneurship, and content creation.

6. ANALYTICS AND TRACKING TOOLS

- **Google Analytics** a powerful tool for tracking website and blog traffic.

- **Google Search Console** Monitors and optimizes how your content appears in Google search results.

- **YouTube Analytics** provides in-depth insights into your video performance.

Remember that the world of content creation is continuously evolving, so staying informed and adapting to new trends and technologies is crucial for long-term success. Use these resources as a foundation, and keep exploring, learning, and innovating in your content creation journey.